PLANNING FOR THE EARLY YEARS

The local community

How to plan learning opportunities that **engage** and **interest** children

By Jennie Lindon

BIRTH TO FIVE

Contents

Published by Practical Pre-School Books, A Division of MA Education Ltd, St Jude's Church, Dulwich Road, Herne Hill, London, SE24 0PB.

Tel: 020 7738 5454

www.practicalpreschoolbooks.com

© MA Education Ltd 2012

Series design: Alison Cutler **fonthill**creative 01722 717043

Series editor: Jennie Lindon

All images © MA Education Ltd. All photos taken by Lucie Carlier.

ISBN 978-1-907241-29-1

Author's acknowledgements:

My warm thanks and appreciation to these settings, who made me so welcome during visits: Crescent I and II Kindergartens (Tooting, South London); Little Learners Nursery School (Skegness); Kennet Day Nursery (Reading); Mary Paterson Nursery School (Queens Park, London); Red Hen Day Nursery (Legbourne) and Southlands Kindergarten and Crèche (Newcastle-under-Lyme). These nurseries are located in very different areas – city, town, coast and rural - and they all use local opportunities to the full. The photos were taken in Mary Paterson Nursery School and Crescent I and II Kindergartens. Thanks also to the team at Tooting Fire Station for their warm welcome. I have waited my entire career to visit a fire station!

Planning to make a difference for children

A child-friendly approach to planning

Young children benefit from reflective adults who plan ahead on the basis of knowing those children: their current interests and abilities, but also what they are keen to puzzle out and learn. Each title in this series of Planning for the Early Years offers a specific focus for children's learning, with activities for you to fine-tune for young girls and boys whom you know well. These adult-initiated activities happen within a day or session when children have plenty of time for initiating and organising their own play. Your focus for the activities is short term; plan ahead just enough so that everything is poised to go.

Thoughtful planning ensures that children enjoy a variety of interesting experiences that will stretch their physical skills, social and communicative abilities, and their knowledge of their own world. A flair for creative expression should be nurtured in early childhood. The national frameworks recognise that creativity is about encouraging open-ended thinking and problem-solving, just as much as opportunities for children to enjoy making something tangible. Plans that make a difference for young children connect closely with their current ability and understanding, yet offer a comfortable stretch beyond what is currently easy.

Adult-initiated activities build on children's current interests. However, they are also planned because familiar adults have good reasons to expect that this experience will engage the children. Young children cannot ask to do something again, or develop their own version, until they have that first-time experience. The best plans are flexible; there is scope for the children to influence the details and adults can respond to what actually happens.

Planning is a process that involves thinking, discussing, doing and reflecting. Young children become part of this process, showing you their interests and preferences by their actions just as much as their words, when spoken language develops. Adult planning energy will have created an accessible, well-resourced learning environment – indoors and outdoors. The suggested activities in this book happen against that backdrop and children's new interests can be met by enhancements to the environment – changes that they can help to organise.

Why explore the local community with young children

The wider world is an intriguing and initially unknown experience for babies and young children. They develop their knowledge and understanding of the world from direct first-hand experiences of their immediate neighbourhood. Over time, young children learn that everyone does not live in the same kind of local community that has become familiar to them. However, any differences, from minor to significant, only make sense on the basis of what has become thoroughly familiar to these young girls and boys.

A considerable amount of what very young children can learn over early childhood makes sense with a firm foundation of local knowledge. For example, the changing seasons are normal weather for the UK. These times of the year are better understood when children are enabled to connect directly with the appearance of the first spring flowers in the local park, as well as opportunities in your garden. Conkers and fallen dried leaves can have many uses: for collections, for display and for creative enterprises. They are best gathered by children themselves from local sources. They make their own choice from the array and realise, perhaps, that this year the conkers are neither very big nor shiny, and wonder why.

It is important to reflect on what happens for young children's learning, if they are not given generous opportunities to become familiar with their local community. How can they become confident independent local travellers later in childhood, if they have had very limited experience of moving around within their own neighbourhood? Young children can be guided during early childhood about taking good care of themselves: the start of a long learning journey about road safety or how to behave wisely on the riverbank.

Thoughtful adults: effective planning

The settings, whose excellent practice helped to inform this book, had leaders and teams who were committed to the value of local outings. They took possible risks seriously, but with a can-do approach, always highlighting the potential benefits for children.

Children will be kept safe – and enabled to learn steadily about keeping themselves safe – by what familiar adults do and say. Your risk assessment and procedures are guidance and a reminder. You need to:

- Obtain written, general permission from parents for their children to take part in local outings that are a normal part of the week. A separate consent form would be needed for special full day trips.

- Make a risk-benefit assessment for each type of local outing: the possible risks that could arise and the ways you will remove or minimise them, including an appropriate adult-child ratio.

- Organise so that any risk assessment sheet is easy for any staff member to check before they leave with a group.

- Review the full assessment about once a year, and ensure that any discussion includes recalling the benefits for children.

- Responsible adult behaviour is to exchange information about local conditions, like blocked roads or paths temporarily closed. You are not expected to re-write the risk assessment for minor changes.

- Consider the most useful reminders to share with children before you go out. Mary Paterson Nursery School has a simple, "We look with our eyes, listen with our ears and think with our head".

- A regular part of local outings is that you will all chat with people you do not yet know. It is not appropriate risk management to warn young children about 'stranger danger' on a regular basis and certainly not each time you step outside.

Children – and adults – need comfortable footwear and suitable clothing for the weather. Set a good example to the children and wear what you say they should, such as a sun hat or gloves. Help children to put on their sun cream in hot summer weather.

The developmental learning journey

The real opportunities within your immediate neighbourhood arise because young children are busy making sense of situations, such as how come adults can get money out of a hole in the wall. Even the older babies start to build a sense of place and space: recognising the last corner before getting back to their childminder's home. You see the ability of even young children to remember, and try to say in words, what happened last time you came to the library. Will the lady with the big puppet be telling stories again? You realise that some young threes understand that people put money into a parking meter machine when they want to park on the street by their playgroup.

The advantage of local trips is that young children use their legs for walking, going up and down steps and running around in larger open spaces. The babies and young toddlers may be in buggies for some trips, but they get out whenever possible, for instance during a trip to the park. I have been part of local outings when three- and four-year-olds were strolling for up to an hour and a half, sometimes also carrying a little bag for their treasures. They were confident walkers, did not moan and had the briefest of sit-downs, if at all.

Of course, you take your time and enable children to build up their stamina. Some over threes may join you who have mainly travelled in a buggy or car seat. Shorter trips, with plenty of interesting sights and happy conversation, will soon have these children surprising their parents with their willingness to walk. A significant pleasure for children is that they have generous attention from the adults. Conversations can flow in the direction that children determine, adults listen and their comments add new ideas and vocabulary in a spontaneous way.

The personal learning journey

Effective planning by adults benefits young children when the ideas for local outings relate closely with the observed interests of children in your home or nursery. Perhaps these toddlers are keen climbers. So, you make sure that local outings include some steps or you know where the fallen tree trunks are

in the local park. You organise to get out to see the flats that are being built locally because cranes, people working and half-finished buildings are always interesting. But maybe you also have some keen builders in the group. Of course, the process can work in the other direction: enjoyable time spent staring at the building site leads to enthusiastic creation of scaffolding back in your garden, and the need for considerably more sticks.

Babies and toddlers feel affirmed as individuals who really matter, when you stop to look at the lorry that has caught their attention. Young children experience a boost to their sense of self-worth when adults are genuinely interested to hear, "My Mummy's friend lives down that road" or they respond to a child's local knowledge of, "That's the police station" as fresh information.

Books and generous play resources are valuable ways for children to learn. However, children should not experience shopping mainly from a book about going to the shops. They should be directly involved in simple, local trips to buy items that are needed. They will then make more sense of a story about buying food or other items. You may also have that delightful experience of watching individual children connect their experience with what they already know. Maybe they return still excited about watching the diggers and dump trucks. The children, perhaps as young as two years of age, go straightaway, pull out their favourite book about big machines and find the picture of the digger to show you.

Children make a difference to adult plans

Young children are dependent on familiar adults to take them out into the neighbourhood. They cannot show their special interests and express curiosity, if they never walk the local routes or if trips are all made at speed to fit an adult agenda.

Once young children are out on a trip into the local community, they can make some choices. Your planning about trips will create a focus for each outing, but relaxed timing means that you can enjoy unexpected events. On a walk to the local park with Mary Paterson Nursery School two children spotted a parked police car. We were having a good look when the police officers returned. They offered for the children to sit in the passenger seat (the car remained parked) and even put on the siren for them. On the way back from a canal walk (with the same nursery) someone spotted a tree surgeon at the top of a very tall tree. We all stood to watch as he sawed off a series of large branches and, in between, waved at us.

Planned activities and specific experiences will be linked with possibilities of what children might learn if they happily engage with this opportunity. When you plan a series of visits to a local park, it is safe to predict that even the youngest children will become more confident walkers, who start to recognise familiar landmarks on the way. They will almost certainly extend their knowledge of plants, flowers and creatures who live in the park. It is very likely that their vocabulary will grow and their ability to have conversations will be enhanced. However, it would be unrealistic to anticipate very specific outcomes, such as which new words they will learn.

Experiences worth talking and thinking about

Even familiar adults cannot be sure what will catch the attention of individual children during the tour of your local church or mosque. Who can know what children will most treasure from today's visit to the fire station? Open-ended planning means that you allow for spontaneous events and what children gain from them. Who knew that the men working on the new water mains in the high road would give such a clear explanation to curious three- and four-year-olds?

If you have the advantage of being in a coastal town, toddlers will show you on a beach trip what has most caught their eye, ear and wish to pick up and explore. Like any other item that is unfamiliar, they may indicate by a quizzical look, or a direct, "What's that?", that they want to know the name of the starfish or the scuttling crab.

Some over threes will surprise you with their general knowledge about creatures at the seaside, park or farm. Out on a shopping trip, you realise that some four-year-olds are already very knowledgeable about how to choose food items and the process of paying for them. Their questions, and what they want to puzzle out, will be different from peers whose family has not made them part of a family shop.

You support children's communication and thinking skills by sharing their current interests, listening to what they want to express and wondering with them about questions that do not have easy answers. The concept of sustained shared thinking describes a joint enterprise between children and adults. You explore together, "I wonder where in the park the stream starts". Or you explore with toddlers, more with actions than words, the different ways to climb up on the fallen log or the most interesting route down this little slope.

Scope for creativity

Of course, you do not plan local outings with a very narrow focus, such as gathering just leaves for a specific kind of leaf printing. A trip to the local open space often benefits from an idea that provides some shape to the outing. Choosing leaves from the park, or shells from the beach, is a starting point for collections that children wish to make and how they choose to use their treasures.

Young children's general knowledge is still partial, although curious girls and boys can be well-informed on the basis of their experience of going to the hairdressers or accompanying a parent to get the MOT done on the family car. Children show intellectual creativity through their questions about what is the difference between a hairdressing salon and a barber's shop. They also make creative guesses about why someone has dug a big hole in the high road – and if there is 'work' going on, then where are the 'workers'?

Children's creativity through pretend play depends on knowledge about their social world. They are very unlikely to be deeply engaged in role play around a post office or travel agency, unless they have spent time inside this facility. Even after a trip, children may be perplexed over quite what happens. Familiar adults will be able to unravel any confusion from what children say during a real visit with you, and by listening to their conversation in the pretend post office.

The creativity of documenting any outings needs to emerge from the children's preferences, as well as your own good ideas. You do not need to document every single trip, let alone every aspect. The children themselves should be part of creating a record that will be enjoyable at the time and for looking at afterwards.

UK frameworks and planning

Early childhood starts with babies and stretches to five or six years of age. Within the four nations of the UK, England is the only country to have moved to a birth to five years framework. Northern Ireland and Scotland have two documents to cover the early years span; Wales currently has a single document. (See page 32 for references.)

However, similar principles within national documents emphasise that:

● Practitioners need to take a personalised approach, supported by flexible planning that takes full account of the current abilities of individual babies and children, as well as likely next steps.

● Young children learn best when there is plenty of scope for child-initiated activities, within a learning environment well resourced for play and friendly conversation.

● Adult-initiated activities should enable children to be mentally and physically active within those experiences and children's interests influence the development of adult plans.

● Headings for aspects of development vary, but the consistent message is that child development is holistic. The areas of learning are presented separately to ensure that nothing is overlooked. Yet, day-by-day, young children, absorbed in an engaging activity, will learn in ways that combine several different areas.

● Children's secure learning depends on practitioners who value, nurture and foster close relationships with children and their family.

Early years practitioners need to be very familiar with their relevant national framework, including the way in which areas of development are organised. Different phrases are used to refer to aspects of children's learning. Yet, there is a consistent emphasis on the central importance of young children's personal, social and emotional development and on building a secure base of communication and spoken language. Along with active respect for children's physical development and wellbeing, these areas of development are the crucial foundations for other areas of young learning.

Wherever early years practitioners live and work, they need to grasp how young children make sense of the early mathematical concepts and how they extend their general knowledge of the wider world. A flair for creative expression should be nurtured in early childhood and the national frameworks acknowledge that creativity is as much about how children think as the pleasure in making something tangible.

The approach to planning, in each national framework, links the key components of:

● Alert observation by practitioners who come to know individual children very well. Observation is a combination of spontaneously noticing what children do and a more planned watching and listening.

- Assessment – a process of making sense – of what has been observed, so that understanding can inform what is offered to individual children and small groups in the immediate and relatively near future.

- Short-term planning shown in adult actions to add resources, so that children can extend their observed interests. Equally short-term, flexible planning for adult-initiated (and maybe adult-led) activities that are likely to engage children and stretch their current abilities or knowledge.

This continual approach is sometimes described as a 'planning cycle', because it is ongoing. Observation, assessment and planning are not separate practitioner activities, each in their own little box. Adult thoughtfulness can be provoked at any point: by what you observe, what you have learned by bringing together your knowledge of this child, and by events within spontaneous play and conversation, or slightly more organised activities. Finally, national early years frameworks raise the importance of children being involved in the process of planning, appropriately for their age. Young children need to be confident that their views and preferences, however expressed, make a difference to what happens day by day.

Making connections with home life

Families living within the same neighbourhood can vary considerably over how much they get out and about with their young children. Early years practitioners, in nursery and the childminding service, notice the difference when they go out on trips in the local community. Some older babies and toddlers show that they anticipate what is across the other side of the now familiar town square. Chatty twos and threes have clear views about what is interesting and should not be missed. Other children are unfamiliar with their local neighbourhood. They have scarcely been to the park, or have only ever been to the swings section. They have never been inside a post office nor chosen vegetables in the market.

Of course, not all families will live in the same neighbourhood as their children go to nursery or childminder's home. It is sometimes easier for working parents to find child care close to their job. Close partnership with parents means that your documentation includes how, "Hamid and his Daddy have brought photos of the market close to their home".

You will communicate your commitment to taking children out and about from your earliest conversations with parents, and other involved family members. They will need to sign the general consent form and that provides an ideal opportunity to describe some recent local trips, including photos. Some families will be delighted that their young sons and daughters will have such a varied experience with you. Other families may initially be surprised that you value such 'ordinary' activities. You need to be ready to explain how the best early education has a very home-like feel, and should not impose a formal classroom structure on young children.

There can be many reasons why some families do not benefit from local opportunities. Parents may feel they have limited time, although some hard-working mothers and fathers still ensure that any weekend activities are built around their children. Perhaps some parents are very focussed on the adult agenda in shopping or other trips. It is possible that their child's experiences with you could open the door to taking a little more time and creating active involvement for young girls and boys. Maybe a family has established very sedentary habits and indoor forms of entertainment. Again, friendly partnership with parents can show that it is not that difficult to get out to the beach, wander through the country park or explore the river towpath.

Within some communities it is expected that women will largely stay within their own home. Respect for diversity within cultural traditions and faith is compatible with a stance that a section of the population should not be highly restricted in their movements just because they are female. A warm invitation to all parents to join specific outings may help some mothers with a justification to go further afield, because involvement is part of their child's early education. Nurseries have sometimes found that mothers then feel more able to repeat this kind of local trip. The same process can help parents who lack self confidence, or who are unrealistically anxious about walking in the local neighbourhood.

Friendly, regular conversation with parents, or involved grandparents, creates an exchange of views about what has interested children, other good ideas and ways in which families have, or would like, to continue at home. This conversation with parents is also the way you discover that a child, who said little on the expedition to track the local stream to its source, nevertheless talked practically non-stop when she got home that afternoon.

Learning about your immediate neighbourhood

Babies, toddlers and young children enjoy simple, local strolls. Your aim is to help them become familiar with the immediate neighbourhood. Think about where you can reach with a buggy push or a round trip walk. A buggy outing could be up to an hour. However, a walking circuit might need to be as short as ten or fifteen minutes, unless you know individual children are already good walkers.

What do you need to do beforehand?

Consider your usual routines and the flow of your day. If you work in a group setting, then the aim is to get a small group out each time. The manager, supported by the whole staff group, needs a practical schedule for the timing of outings and which day or days of the week are best. In my visits to Southlands Crèche I saw the baby room team walk out with the buggies almost every day; it took seriously bad weather to stop them. Sometimes babies will doze off in their buggy; sometimes they will be fully awake and alert to the sights.

Childminders often do a drop-off and a pick-up of children at reception class or primary school. These daily events may be ideal for making the outward or return trip more of a meandering time, even if not every day. Nurseries with a similar commitment can take a few younger children on the walk to pick up the older children. I have known teams who ensured that this routine trip was an event of interest to the younger children, who enjoyed the conversation on the way.

Consider the highlights of your neighbourhood. Have you got a good vantage point for looking at the trains or a local garden with an impressive array of gnomes? Where is the best place for watching the dust cart on rubbish pick up day?

Even the babies realise that you stop and look with them when something has caught their eye. Toddlers in the buggy or slow walking twos come to know that you are as interested as them to watch the squirrel balancing along the fence. Over a week, take out small groups at a time. Depending on the age of walking children, you probably need two children to each adult. You hold hands and it is easy to chat with children. The chance for personal conversation is lost if you use a walking device with many children holding onto handles. The point of a local outing is to relish the stroll, including the walk to get somewhere in particular. The aim is not to move efficiently and at speed.

An opportunity to learn about the local community

This circuit can become the basis of what you do regularly. Young children's understanding of the wider

world has to be grounded in their personal sphere. Even before they express their knowledge in spoken words, young children show their growing recognition of familiar sights. A three-year-old may say, "This is our street", yet a 18 month old will look with recognition or point to the big tree by the front door of her childminder. Even the youngest children show their particular interest in the café with the fancy tables and umbrellas close to nursery. Over threes may request a route that goes by the special hedge with the fancy shapes on top.

You and the children will get to know some people within a regular local circuit: the person who runs the corner shop or a neighbour in the same road who regularly tends the front garden. Even very young children start to recognise these familiar faces and, accompanied by you, are happy to give a cheery, "Hallo". You will enable young children to build a sense that people in the neighbourhood should be friendly in return.

Part of learning about personal safety for children is that most adults mean well; a blunt 'stranger danger' message is unhelpful in the long run. The babies in the buggy and young children holding your hand will eventually move about on their own. They need to understand that other people in the neighbourhood should be friendly and willing to help out, if necessary.

Responding to children and babies' interests

Young children have to be in a comfortable position to be able to express an interest in what they can see or hear.

Babies will benefit most from being in the style of buggy where they face the adult pushing. They can sleep in peace but can also see you clearly, when they are wakeful, and want to have a 'chat'. People disagree about the best age to switch to a buggy when the seat faces outwards, with the child facing away from the pusher. The best approach is to watch a child's behaviour. Some young toddlers, but also some older babies, show that they really want to see what you see. Double buggies should have both children on the same level, so they can see properly.

Listening to children and talking with them

Early childhood is a powerful time for learning. Babies, toddlers and young children are ready to be delighted by sights that the grown-ups find so familiar that they scarcely notice any more. So, never assume that a very ordinary local sight (to you) could not be fresh and of serious interest to a young child.

Babies use their senses to listen to sounds and watch what passes by their line of vision. You 'listen' to what babies' gestures tell you and what they 'say' by the direction in which they stare. It is important to get regularly on the same eye level as babies and young toddlers in a buggy. You need to connect directly with their line of sight and interest. You can, of course, point out things of interest in your turn. In the same way, you get on the same eye level as walking older toddlers and young children.

Young toddlers and slightly older children are fascinated by the natural world: stones, leaves, squirrels, snails. They need local trips that have time to stand and stare. Young children are soon fascinated by their glimpses into the adult world: why are those men digging up the high street and where does the post van take all those letters from the post box? Children build their general knowledge when familiar adults listen carefully and answer those questions which individual children want to ask today.

Learning about the wider local community

This suggestion is a development from the basic local circuit. If you have needed to coax children to get walking, then add another five minutes with each subsequent walk. Your aim is to get older toddlers and over twos used to the idea that walking is an enjoyable and normal way to get from one place to another. Everyone has sights, for free, within local walking distance. It is valuable for young children to enjoy outings that cost nothing and do not involve always getting into a car.

Do you have different kinds of shops or a market? What are the possibilities of your nearest green open space in an urban area, or accessible, public land in a more rural area? If your nursery is in a country district, have you found good viewing places for watching farm animals? Red Hen Day Nursery was able to take children on rambles across their own extensive land. Other rural nurseries will need to identify the nearby public footpaths that criss-cross private land.

Towns and cities have a wide range of birds and daytime creatures like squirrels in even quite small green spaces. Where is your nearest post box, or do you have a post office in walking distance? Who would think it would be worth stopping at the undertakers' window on the high street? Yet, they have a little fountain which enchants children. What are the temporary events that will be worth a stroll to investigate, like the front garden with the enormous sunflowers?

What do you need to do beforehand?

Maybe one or two children show interest in the post box or glance into the post office on your high street. Your next outing could be to buy some stamps. Then take your time with children (over twos will manage this) and support them to choose a drawing that will be placed in an envelope addressed to each child's family. Fours and over may wish to 'write a message' as well. Help children to place the stamp correctly on the envelope. Then you go out to post their letters.

I joined the small group trips from Crescent I Kindergarten to post their letters. The children who could walk a little further went to the post office; the other groups walked to the post box. The team leader had popped into the post office the previous day to tell them about the visit. The staff were very welcoming and happy for the children to have a good look at the weighing machines and how to pay by credit card.

It will not always be necessary or appropriate to say in advance that you will be coming by with a small group of children. You may judge it is wise to have a chat with young children about "We walk, we don't run" when inside the garden centre. But you should not have to ask permission to take children into local shopping facilities.

An opportunity to learn about the broader neighbourhood

The great advantage of walking the same or similar local routes is that even the youngest children build a mental map of the immediate neighbourhood. You support children's curiosity because you are interested as well. Today, you have turned a corner and there is the market, but you have approached from the other end.

Once children start to recognise a familiar landmark, like the church steeple close to your home, you can invite them to join in the walking navigation. Can they recall which way you now turn to get back to base? Some young boys and girls will be able to make a choice between different routes for the return journey. Maybe a brief look into the local garden centre becomes a firm request to return. They are intrigued by the many water features, as well as the plants.

Young children are ready to be intrigued by very 'ordinary' sights and regular events. Why are there piles of black plastic bags or large wheelie bins on the street? Today is the day that household rubbish is collected. Why are some bags orange (or whatever colour)? People are supposed to put their recycling into different bags.

Responding to children and babies' interests

You will have familiarised yourself with the different local routes, but the children may be enthused about planning a route with you. Maybe a couple of four-year-olds remind you about the route that is better, because today you have two toddlers in the double buggy. Perhaps some children like to walk up the slope to the park, rather than the steps.

As over threes become intrigued about what is where locally, create a simple, large size map. With children's involvement, mark the nursery, children's homes or the park and a few significant landmarks. Over fives understand more about small scale representation of a familiar area. So they may be ready to create their own layout, with some help. Can you obtain an aerial photo of your neighbourhood? Children and parents will be intrigued by this very different perspective.

Reflect on your own experience of these first local trips, especially if you have been used to a higher level of adult structure in any activity. Are you planning on the basis that children must keep having 'new' activities? Yet, they enjoy and definitely benefit from doing the same, or a very similar trip again. Older twos, and certainly the threes and older, will sometimes recall the last time in words. Maybe they want to reminisce with you about how it is odd that the garden centre is also called a 'nursery'. Are you leaving the trip and timing flexible so children can make some active choices on the basis of their personal past experience?

Listening to children and talking with them

It is striking that young children, even the quieter ones, often start to chat as you walk along at the beginning of a local outing. They are immediately interested in the sights. But it may also be significant that one adult is likely to be walking with only a few children, maybe one to each hand. This adult can give full attention to whatever the children want to say. Maybe a child calls your attention to the number 6 big red bus. This double decker is his very own bus, because that brings him and his parent to nursery each day.
The very youngest children will have limited language, so you are alert to their gaze and any words. Is this toddler looking intently at the cyclist? You can respond with, "Yes I can see! It's a man on a bicycle". You will often not speak the home language of children who are in the process of learning English. Does this three-year-old point to the police car that is zooming along the road? You can respond with, "What a noise! It's a police car. I wonder where they're going?"

Of course, you do not only listen: you make a contribution to the conversation. Maybe you call children's attention to the sounds of the trains over head, as you walk under the railway bridge. Is there an echo to enjoy in this part of the pedestrian subway that takes you under the big roundabout? Can you hear the sounds of the big ships in the harbour, although you are some distance away?

Learning about going to the local shops

Plan an outing with a small group of children in which you will walk to your nearest shop or shops and make a purchase. This activity is suitable for younger children, although the babies and very young toddlers will be in a buggy. Even two-year-olds can hand over the money to buy the cress seeds from your local garden centre. You will help very young children as they move towards understanding this process.

What do you need to do beforehand?

Childminders will look at the daily routine. Today it makes sense for you and the younger children to buy a range of fruit on the way to the school pick-up for the older children. You can all make a fruit salad tomorrow. In a group setting you plan jointly with colleagues, so that small groups of children can get out throughout the week.

What are the pedestrian skills of the children you plan to take? Will they be able to walk to the market and back? Can a couple of older children be trusted to hold hands together, without an adult? They can walk in the middle of your group, with an adult, plus two children in front and another set behind. Have a store of small, robust bags that will allow children to carry purchases back. Or else have a shopping trolley for this purpose; a child can probably tow it until it is loaded with shopping.

Very young children may be keen to walk but will get tired. One child may have a physical disability or health problem that means a buggy needs to be available. Organise a timing that enables this child to walk some of the way. You will have asked for a general permission from all parents, but you may have further conversations when families have special concerns about their son or daughter.

It is useful to have a specific purpose for some local trips. Today you might plan to buy fresh bread from the bakery or vegetables from the market. Perhaps you explain to the children that this morning you will all go to the supermarket and buy the ingredients for making blueberry muffins this afternoon. Around Halloween there will be some impressive displays of pumpkins in the shops. Children may already have seen some carved into shapes, but are unaware that you can eat this vegetable. Maybe you can make some pumpkin soup or a pie today.

You share the plan in advance with the children, even the youngest who understand only some of what you say. The advantage of explaining what you are all going to do is that young children sometimes start to ask you questions on the way, about what and why and where. Of course, your main aim of making a purchase still allows time for spontaneous events, like watching the huge stag beetle crossing the path.

An opportunity to learn about shopping with a purpose

Children benefit from the opportunity to talk with you and each other before the outing. Perhaps they need some material to make superhero cloaks, so the plan is to go to the shop on the high street that sells material and haberdashery. Is someone going to make a note of what is needed? Young children develop emergent writing though opportunities to make marks that have a purpose, such as a shopping list. Visits to shops and market stalls offer opportunities for children themselves to ask for "Two bananas, please" or "Have you got any crusty rolls?"

Real money is a baffling concept to young children, as is the idea of getting change from the shopkeeper, when more money is handed over than the price of the goods. Make sure that children are involved in the planning that "We need to take some money". They should be offered an active part in making a choice, checking or asking about prices and the actual purchase.

Responding to children and babies' interests

Do they need more resources for list-making and little bags?

Perhaps several children lingered by the delicatessen counter. They had no idea that there were so many kinds of cheese and that they each have names. Would they be interested to organise a tasting session

and invite their parents? The children are impressed with the fresh bread for tea and like your suggestion that, "We could bake our own bread". Young children do not necessarily realise that you can make many foods rather than buy them in shops.

Perhaps your main aim was to buy the ingredients for making vegetable soup later in the day. You help children to search for the ingredients on the shopping list. But there is time for them to point out fruit that they recognise or items that are unfamiliar.

Listening to children and talking with them

Going out to make a purchase can become a regular event; it is not an activity to do once and never again. Once the walking route is familiar to children, you can encourage recall with, "Which way do we turn to get to the market (or high street)?"

Perhaps you are going to more than one shop – all with a purpose that makes sense to young children. Over threes soon want to recap with you, "First we went to the supermarket to buy everything for our cake. Then we posted the letters. Then we came back past Nathan's house".

Of course, you respond to children's comments and questions. But you can ask questions appropriate to the outing, like, "How many carrots do we need? Will you count them for me?" or, "We need blueberries to make our muffins. Now what do blueberries look like?" You explain that loose fruit needs to be placed carefully in the basket or trolley, otherwise it may bruise. Children may be alert to fruit or vegetables that already have marks. You may decide together that small imperfections are not a problem, because you will cut them out, when you make your fruit salad or soup.

Sometimes (not always) when you are five minutes away from nursery, let a child use your work mobile phone (with you for emergencies) to say, "We're nearly back".

Learning about going to the park (or other open green space)

Young children will enjoy generous time in your own outdoor area. They will still benefit from experiencing other, different outdoor environments. Plan a trip to your nearest park, common or other public green space. The first visits can be just to see what is there and for toddlers and children to be able to run about in a larger space than even the largest nursery garden. Some parks have a play area for young children. You can allow for some time in that section, but the park outing is not exclusively to go on the swings.

What do you need to do beforehand?

You need to know this open green space well: the features and the boundaries. A common may be accessible from almost any point. However, some parks will have a boundary fence or wall, with entrance gates. Can you create a good route by entering by one way and leaving by a different gate? You can spot features that will almost certainly delight young children: the log that you lift up to see the creepy-crawlies underneath, or the weeping willow that will be a safe hiding and peep-boo place. Children will show you their interests on the day, but you will be able to make some good guesses.

Of course, walking children will hold your hand along the pavement or path to reach the park. The delight of a safe open space is that children do not have to hold on any more. However, every adult knows the location of the children who are her/his responsibility today. Any parent helpers or students need to know that they keep an active eye on each of their assigned children for the whole trip.

Babies and toddlers can travel to the park in a buggy. Very young children need to conserve their energy for when you have reached the park. Over threes, some older twos, can walk to and from the park. Build up their stamina slowly, if necessary, with shorter local walks.

The local park can become a very special place for young children, with favourite corners and sights that they like to see each time. You take seriously what young children create around favourite outdoor places. If they think baby dragons live in this little shaded area of the park, then follow that imaginary leap with them. However, children need to take the lead on any pretending. It is not for the adults to try to initiate a fantasy by claiming to see elves or hiding alleged fairy items to be discovered.

An opportunity to learn about the environment of your local park

At some times of the year there will be opportunities for collecting, for instance, dry leaves, twigs, conkers or acorns. Children enjoy having their own little bags for such treasures. It is worth collecting the small but tough deli bags which are given for carrying bought coffee and sandwiches. Babies enjoy looking and pointing to choose. Toddlers are ready to pick their own items and put them into their own bag. You will have a table, shelf or top of a low storage cupboard ready for children to lay out their treasures.

Once children are confidently mobile, they gain confidence when they can venture a little bit away from familiar adults, in a larger outdoor space than the majority of gardens. You will still be close enough so that even the toddlers can safely stretch the invisible elastic connecting them to familiar and trusted adults.

Young children benefit from being active in the preparations for any outing. Toddlers learn to fetch their outdoor coat and shoes, although they will need help in getting these on. Learning the skills of self-care is an important task for early childhood, and some children have special health issues. Yet, four- and five-year-olds can take an active part in remembering their own inhaler, with adult support. Some over threes are already good organisers and like to be part of final checks, such as whether you have got the blanket, so the baby can be comfortable on the grass. Or they may well remind you how you forgot the camera last time.

Responding to children and babies' interests

What catches the attention of the babies or toddlers? In dry weather you can lay out a thick blanket for sitting babies, or put them on their stomach. What do they see, what seems to get them to pause and listen? Perhaps they like to watch the waving branches, so you need a spot where they can lie on their back and look (clearly not looking into the sunlight.) Babies and children love to watch feathers or leaves float down and try to get the sycamore 'helicopters' to spin. Throw some of these items up in the air for them. Maybe you anticipated that the toddlers would love to clamber on the fallen tree trunks. But they surprised you with their interest in the bandstand.

Time for you to think

Are you striking the right balance between safety and freedom for children? They need to explore the park actively in order to learn. You can guide them over what and how 'we touch', but they will have a very limited experience, if adults take a no-touching approach. Carrying a store of wet wipes will deal with clean-enough hygiene.

Perhaps children became intrigued by trees and bark. So, next time you could bring magnifying glasses. Did the children become interested in what they spotted high in a tree or at a distance? Maybe next time you could bring some binoculars.

Listening to children and talking with them

Babies may have a favourite spot to which they want to return. They will show you by their eye movements and pointing. Older toddlers will make it clear by gestures and a few words that it is very important to go via the flower bed with the funny little fence or here is the big tree that they like to run round very fast. Long before they understand much about growth, very young children will delight in watching how signets grow into swans, over a series of outings to the pond in your local park pond.

As children's speech extends, then they will use their words to direct your attention. "Look, look!" will start the conversation that flows when one or two children spot a squirrel up high in the tree and then, great excitement, there is another one. Your natural use of vocabulary will extend the words that they later use: up high, on the next branch, hanging on tight, spinning around and other phrases. Some children will need several go's at the word 'squirrel'; the opening combination sound is not that easy. Also, younger children may need your help when they want to share this experience with their parents at the end of the day.

Children's questions or questioning comments are the best opportunity for you to share some information about the changing seasons. Be ready for any chance for you all to ask a gardener or park keeper, "Where have the rose bushes gone?"

Learning about water in the natural environment

Young children are interested in water in its many forms. They will have fun with water in your garden. However, there is a special kind of excitement about large stretches of water, whether that is a pond, lake or the moving water of a stream, river or canal. If you live on the coast, then your accessible water comes with a sandy or pebbly beach. Organise a local outing where the main focus is to experience and explore a stretch of water.

What do you need to do beforehand?

You need to check on the ways to access the canal or the riverbank. For instance, where are the access points from the nearby road? Are these steps or slopes, so are some access points better for the group that goes out with babies and toddlers in buggies? Perhaps there is continuous access to the stream that meanders through the park, although there is an especially good view from one of the pedestrian bridges.

Will the children be fine in ordinary shoes or will this trip require wellington boots? You will have checked that the temporary 'wetlands' on the common are very shallow, because you walked through the area thoroughly in your boots. This depth of this temporary watery environment will be ideal for children to wade about. A store of sticks and markers will be very handy for them to test the depth, if they wish. You can still demonstrate to children how to move slowly into the wet area, to check as you go.

What kind of beach is available on your coastline and how do the tides affect the environment for young children? Is the beach equally accessible from low tide through to high tide? Alternatively, do you need to check the tides because there is very little beach left at high tide?

What kind of water have you got within walking distance? Is there a pond or small lake in your nearest park? Is there a river, stream or canal with an accessible towpath? Maybe there are areas on your local common which are usually dry. Yet, they become waterlogged after heavy rain and children will be intrigued about this significant change to a familiar landscape. So long as you have the adults to take a child to each hand, then twos and older will enjoy this trip – depending on the length of the walk to get to the water.

If you are on the coast, then plan ways to take children to the beach. I was able to join the regular beach afternoon for a small group of over threes in Little Learners Nursery School. You can experience the features of your specific stretch of coast: sand or pebbles, perhaps groynes and other sea defence systems, maybe a river entering the sea and seaside creatures like crabs or starfish.

An opportunity to learn about water within the natural environment

When children experience a local stretch of water, they become interested in the flow of moving water or the ripples that can build up even on a small pond, when there is a breeze. Think about how you will explain the phenomenon of tides on your beach, as well as why the sea is sometimes full of lively waves and sometimes very calm. You may find a well illustrated book. It is also well worth checking the Internet for visual explanations that can be found, for example, in educational YouTube videos.

When you and the children visit at different times of the year, you will all see how this lake or landscaped water feature in the park changes. Maybe this pond freezes in winter or the stream level rises when there has been a long wet period. In contrast, what happens in times of drought? Maybe you go to see the little waterfall in the park and, to your disappointment, there is no water flow at all. Perhaps a notice, which you read out to the children, explains that the pump does not work if the water gets too low.

Responding to children and babies' interests

Children may be most intrigued by how the water moves in the steam. Can they toss leaves or twigs

into the flow? The babies will watch, and you hold them up to see the ducks or the rowing boats on the lake. Walking toddlers and young children may be keen to follow the path that goes around the small lake. They can be intrigued by the different viewpoints.

On the beach today maybe the children want to collect small rocks and strand of seaweed. Before you know it, large scale outdoor art is being created by three- and four-year-olds. Beach creations are inevitably temporary, so you can offer the option of taking photos.

when it leaves the park or whether the stream has a name. Think with the children how you could answer these questions. Some children might be especially interested in why this patch of common is usually dry but sometimes it gets very wet? The reason may be that there is an underground stream. How can we find out?

Perhaps part of the interest of this stretch of canal or narrow river is that narrow boats are moored along one stretch. You can share the information that this kind of boat is someone's home. Then you follow what children want to comment or ask. It might be why do some people want to live on a boat, do the boats ever move or does that cat actually live there too? Of course, you do not necessarily know all the answers. Can you ask someone on one of the boats?

Learning about eating out in the local community

You can provide young children with the experience of different kinds of food – for snack, lunch or teatime. Young boys and girls also benefit from learning how to prepare simple meals and basic cooking skills. A further valuable experience can be for children to eat out in a local café. Plan an outing to somewhere in walking distance and take a small number of children. If you work in group provision, you can steadily take out all the children over time – not necessarily to the same place. This outing is probably for over threes, although you may have some older twos who will manage.

Perhaps your local delicatessen is mostly used for buy and take away, but they also offer a lunchtime menu to eat there. Perhaps the Turkish bakery is known across your town as the place to get wonderful pastries and they have placed a few tables on their section of the pavement. You might choose the café or small restaurant because they have a local speciality on their menu. Of course, you do not want to break the budget, but the food can be economical, maybe Cornish pasties or Staffordshire oatcakes.

Some young children have been nowhere other than fast food chains. No offence to this option; it is useful sometimes. However, it is valuable to extend their experience to places where customers are served at the table and are provided with plates, glasses and cutlery appropriate to the meal.

What do you need to do beforehand?

Check out local places where the menu has items that will be suitable for you and the children for a light lunch, snack or teatime treat. Review whether children have any family preferences over diet, or food allergies, that mean you need to double-check items on the menu of your first choice.

You would not necessarily tell the café you are coming and certainly not ask, as if they are doing you a favour to serve adults with young children. However, if the best place is often busy, it could be a wise idea to reserve a table for your small group this afternoon. The idea of having your own table reserved for you is likely to be a novelty to young children.

You may have a fund for small purchases. Perhaps families could contribute a small sum to the snack or afternoon tea. Maybe a parent or grandparent can be invited to join the outing.

Have you considered yet an effective way to show who has left the nursery to go out on a trip? For example, Mary Paterson Nursery School has a special "Who is out?" board on which children and adults put their photo on leaving and then, when they return, put the photos back on the main board for who is in nursery today.

An opportunity to learn about a real café or restaurant

The language and intellectual development of two-year-olds should have progressed to the point where they are able to play around with their knowledge of how the world works. You see the emergence of simple pretend play with these still very young children. Then, over the year that they are three, girls and boys weave the more complex pretend of role play.

Perhaps some children have set up a pretend café on the basis of their experiences within their own family. Yet, some young boys and girls struggle to play pretend customers and café owners, because they have never visited a real café or little restaurant. Young children can only imagine variations around real experiences that they have already had within their life. Twos, who are keen to join the pretend café, need a clear steer from the more knowledgeable threes and fours.

A relaxed meal or snack in a café can help young children understand how to behave in this kind of venue. Together you will find a table, sit down, and make choices from a menu or a counter display. They experience how everyone remains sitting, chats to each other and maybe looks around. At some point, most likely at the end of the meal, you (or one of the children) will ask for the bill and pay.

Responding to children and babies' interests

Kennet Day Nursery surprised their local pizza restaurant with how much three- and four-year-olds already knew about making their own pizzas and the questions they therefore wanted to ask. In general, when children understand more about how a café works, they are better equipped to set up or extend their pretend version.

Were children intrigued about what goes on behind the scenes? In some local cafes it is possible to watch as the counter staff make sandwiches, brew coffee or bring out the bun that you have chosen. In other places the cooking and food preparation happens in another room and full plates appear with the waiter or waitress.

Once you have made friendly contact with a local restaurant they might be happy to invite children to look at the kitchen when it is not in full swing. An alternative is that some restaurant chains will organise a tour.

Time for you to think

As you reflect on the outing, you learn more about individual children. Was the idea of a menu a new idea to some children? Did some know enough to ask, "What does that say?" Or perhaps one child queried, "Where are the pictures?", because he was familiar with illustrated menus. It may be a novel idea to some children that once you have made your choice in a café, you cannot change it, unless you are very swift. Even if children understand some written numbers, it is not necessarily obvious that numbers on a menu – card or board – tell customers the price of items.

Listening to children and talking with them

A visit to a café or small restaurant will show you the differences between individual children: what they understand and what puzzles them. Perhaps some ask a lot of questions about what is inside pies or flans, whereas another child is attracted by nice icing and decorations. Conversation flows alongside enjoyment of the food, but there will be opportunities for you to use vocabulary appropriate to this meal and to the eating out experience. Specific words for different types of cake or bread will arise naturally, as well as questions about unfamiliar ingredients. Encourage children to direct some of their questions to the café owner or waitress. Even young children can gain the confidence to ask for apple pie but without any custard.

In a small café or deli the children may be able to watch most of the food preparation. They may be intrigued by use of food tongs and want to know why these are used. Or they notice that the person making up your wraps is wearing plastic gloves, rather like those you wear when you change the baby. If the kitchen is out of sight, then some children may ask where do people make all this food.

Children may ask questions within this outing about the whole business of payment. They wonder about who you are supposed to pay or how you know what the baked potato costs.

Learning about a local service

Most of your local outings can be open-ended trips, with a flexible goal. Children will then enjoy a few events, when you have made a specific arrangement to visit somewhere. You could make contact with different places of worship in your local area and get a sense of their experience of chatting with and showing round a group of young children. Fire officers spend a lot of shifts with no emergency call-out and their fire station manager will almost certainly have a community education focus.

Maybe you have enthusiastic runners in your group, who are regularly doing speedy circuits of the garden. Mary Paterson Nursery School took their children to spend the afternoon running on the local athletics track. Have you got such a facility in the local park or common? You can always ask; the worst that can happen is a "No".

You need to plan this more organised visit from what you can reasonably predict the children will understand. Under twos will not have enough general knowledge to make much sense of this kind of visit. However, in a childminder's mixed age group, the baby or young toddler will find something to catch their eye. A few older twos may understand some aspects, but over threes are more likely to connect the new experience with their current knowledge in some ways.

What do you need to do beforehand?

Given the size of the vet's surgery, what would be a sensible number for the group? A visit to the vet's requires a double check on whether any children (or accompanying adults) are allergic to any animals. Such allergies can be triggered by small amounts of fur or hair.

I visited the local fire station with the children of Crescent II Kindergarten. Several years ago, the team leader had a full meeting with the station manager for their first ever visit.

The fire station team are used to visits from young children and have a well-tested pattern of what they do with a group. This successful outing became an annual event and now all that is needed is to make contact, refresh information and set a date.

You can anticipate what the environment will seem like to children. Given the size of the vet's surgery, what would be a sensible limit to numbers in the group? You need to do your own risk assessment, with your age range of children in mind. Will you need family volunteers to ensure enough adults for this trip? If so, then allow enough time to send out a letter and get replies for parents or grandparents who can join you.

An opportunity to learn about a local facility

Good ideas for special local visits may also evolve from family events which children share with you and their friends. For instance, one child may have a new pet dog, or another child's cat may have been ill and the vet made him better. These would be timely reasons to call the local vet and discuss the possibility of bringing a small group out on a visit. Professionals like vets or dentists are sometimes happy to visit a nursery, but children do not then see the actual place of work.

Public services or places of worship are often themselves keen to build strong links with the local community. Emergency services like fire and police want children to build a positive view of what this profession does for the community. Medical services like the health clinic or dental surgery, or facilities like a vet's practice recognise that young children can start to learn about their own health or taking good care of their pet.

Responding to children's interest in the fire station

If children are already interested in fire engines, you may set up a role play fire station area before your visit. You are seeking a balance between helping children to be ready for what they will experience, yet leave plenty of scope for responding afterwards with resources, linked with their specific interests. A well illustrated information book will help you to prime children's expectations about what they are likely to see. Children will then make more sense of the fire officers' protective clothing or why they need a mask and torch. Were children most taken with having a go with the fire hose (with a fire officer holding on tight)? Did the safety message about heat and fire provoke some questions later? You could extend children's understanding through first-hand experiences such as building a simple outdoor fire pit or buying a proper fire bowl. For ideas see www.mindstretchers.co.uk

Listening to children and talking with them

In what way do children express a direct interest in following up their visit to the fire station? Are some children keen to create their own 'really big' fire engine out of recycled materials – now they understand the size of the vehicle, having stood next to the real thing. Now they will welcome your reminder of what they saw during the visit, for instance how the fire engine did not have seat belts like a car, but a special harness to hold each fire officer secure. Perhaps some children were a little over-awed at the time, but your photos will provoke conversation now.

Children do not necessarily want to weave their experience at the vet's into pretend play. They may be more interested to browse the books you have about different animals. Or they enjoy replaying their visit to the dentist's through comparing it with the story in the illustrated book. Children's choice of information books will enable them and you to revisit how the special dentist's chair changes so you lie flat, or how the dentist had big and little mirrors.

What do children spontaneously recall about the peaceful atmosphere of the mosque or the beautiful patterns? Were they struck by the flower displays in the church? Perhaps they want a reminder that the huge thing with the pipes is called an organ. Maybe nobody was playing during your visit and you could find a CD of organ music.

Learning to use a local facility (the library or museum)

Even if you have a generous store of books for children to enjoy, it is still well worth planning a trip with them to your local library. If you live in a rural area, your version may be to organise a visit from the mobile library.

With a small group of children, you can simply drop in to the library. If you are taking a larger group of children, it is courteous to book a visit. If for no other reason, another group might visit at the same time and make life a bit crowded. Other possibilities could include a local museum within walking distance, or a shop or café which features the work of local artists. You are seeking facilities that are free, or which do not charge entrance to young children and accompanying adults. Both Mary Paterson Nursery School and the Crescent Kindergartens take groups of children to an art gallery, which includes a trip on public transport.

You can judge the length of your visit because you are familiar with individual children. You may decide to keep the first library visit relatively short and have a plan of the shelf to which you will introduce this group of young twos and threes. They may feel overwhelmed by the choice of books, without some friendly guidance. You could organise the first visit to the local museum, having planned which room, or even which few items you and the children will go to see. You can make an informed decision on the basis of what you know interests familiar children, or is likely to engage them.

What do you need to do beforehand?

Check on the opening times of the library or art gallery. An initial visit, without the children, will enable you to walk the physical environment. Is the children's library on the ground floor, or will you need to take children upstairs or in a small group in the lift? Familiarise yourself with the children's section: how is it organised by age bands or types of book and what are the seating/browsing arrangements. Does the library have some regular events – which might also be of interest to the children, but would not be a good time for a browsing visit?

In a similar way, you can have a practical conversation with customer liaison at the museum or art gallery. Explain that you will be bringing a group of young children and how you plan a manageable focus for them. Any local facility of this kind should be welcoming to children, as current and future users of this service. You may purchase a postcard of an item on display, or of a painting, that you think would best interest the children.

An opportunity to learn about the library or museum

An important part of young children's learning journey towards literacy is their growing love of books: story books (fiction) but also information books (non-fiction). Your local library will offer children the opportunity to browse among a far wider range of books than you will have, even in the largest nursery. Some children own their own books and see their parents reading. However, some families have few, if any, books at home. Young children need to experience that they can borrow a wide range of books from the library, with the hope that they might want to continue with the support of parents, or later as older, independent borrowers.

If you organise regular trips, children begin to understand, or extend what they have grasped about the concept of lending and borrowing. You will be supporting even the youngest children to take good care of shared possessions, including those on short term loan from somewhere else. You will help children with this consideration if the library books are kept in a separate, labelled container accessible, but with that visual reminder of their source.

When you have borrowed something, children can be helped to understand a bit more about the passing of time. You could usefully explore a way to have a visual memory jogger for everyone about when this batch of books needs to go back. The same approach could work well if you borrow play resources from a toy library. Perhaps you could write a note in your flexible plan for the week, with a suitable picture or logo.

Responding to children's interest in the museum or gallery

You can prepare children by sharing the postcard of the painting, or an image of the display, that you will all look at first. During the actual visit, see what catches children's attention. What do they indicate, by looking or words, that they feel is most interesting about the Viking helmet or the old photos of the high street? They may admire the painting of the orchard but, back at nursery, they want to recreate the vibrant abstract painting.

Did you prepare children well for the visit? Did they have accurate expectations about seeing photos of your local park 'in the old days'. Maybe the children benefited from being familiar with the style of Turner's paintings. They were so excited to spot them across the gallery room.

Did you and the children discover unexpected exhibits in the museum; is it definitely worth another visit? Are some children more able to cope with reasonably peaceable behaviour in a public place? Do the children who struggled need a friendly reminder about using their 'indoor voice'.

Listening to children and talking with them

Public libraries are peaceful, but not silent places. So, of course, young children can comment and ask questions. Some children may be more interested in what the grown-ups are doing in the adult section: on computers, reading newspapers or books, or perhaps studying. You can satisfy children's curiosity by a joint wander around the shelves for adults.

As they talk about the details of visiting the library, children may use, or welcome your introduction of vocabulary like borrow, check-out, library card and you can explain the difference between fiction and non-fiction. Some children will already have favourite books. You can help them search for other books by the same author, talking them through a basic version of alphabetical filing.

A local museum or art gallery is not a run-around-and-shout place like the park. However, children can still talk in their normal voices, not hushed tones. If you have some lively chatters, who are still discovering volume control, then remind them of the difference between your 'indoor voice' and your 'outdoor one'. The new vocabulary will depend on the exhibit or painting on which you focus, or which captured children's attention. It may be a new idea to children that you could all look for more paintings by the same person, as you have for books in the library. Can you follow up a local painter or sculptor, maybe invite them for a visit to nursery?

Learning about a special local event

The enjoyment of special local events is that you and the children connect with other people and places in your neighbourhood. Check out what happens, and when within the year, for events at a realistic walking distance of your provision. You might also consider an event that is a short bus or tram ride away. A journey into town or another part of the city may bring more possibilities.

What do you need to do beforehand?

Are there regular annual events, such as the arrival of the winter lights display on the lampposts along your high street? You might plan to walk to the charity shop that always has the best special displays and see what they have done this time for Halloween, or for Easter. Organise to see special displays in the local church and to ask the vicar to chat with the children about this particular event in the faith calendar.

Under fives will be too young for many events in a local book/literary festival or an Eisteddfod. Check out whether there will be a story teller or poetry suitable for your children, or singing and dancing events with audience participation. Explore the history of this particular local event. How many years has there been an Eisteddfod, or special games, in your town?

Maybe the carnival, that children believe has 'always' happened, was not established in their parents' childhood. On the other hand, children might assume that this year is the first ever May Day celebration. Find images and information from your library, museum or local history society. If some families have lived in the area for generations, then grandparents will be able to share their reminiscences.

Extend your knowledge of what happens locally. Some longstanding special events like May Day could potentially happen anywhere in the UK, although every area does not choose to organise this celebration. Some special events have never spread across the whole country. For instance, well dressing is an established tradition in Derbyshire, and also in Yorkshire and Staffordshire http://www.historic-uk.com/CultureUK/WellDressing.htm

Celebrations and festivals make more sense to young children when there is a personal connection: their family, the family of their friend or a familiar location. Is there a large enough local Chinese community that Chinese New Year celebrations actually happen in your streets? Do you have a carnival time that is not too crowded for young children, or a local event that involves dressing up and a few floats? There will be special times of the year when decorations go up temporarily in your area. It may be Christmas decorations in the shops or a tree in a front garden beautifully draped with twinkly lights.

Fireworks

An opportunity to learn about a special local event

The aim of this activity is to become part of a celebration or tradition that children can actually see locally. Early understanding of cultural traditions is best led by first-hand experiences for young children, rather than books about people and places they cannot meet or visit. Babies and under-threes will enjoy the sights and sounds, as will over threes. You would not expect even five- or six-year-olds to gain a sophisticated understanding of the ideas behind Diwali, or other celebrations linked with a world faith. Your aim is that young children have an enjoyable experience and are able to make sense of a family-oriented event, that is happening in their neighbourhood.

Young children will understand only some of the historical background to May Day. However, they are likely to be interested in an event like this, that has been celebrated for a very long time. Full scale maypole dancing will be too difficult. But they could enjoy learning some very simple ribbon dancing and then watching older children or adults perform the more complex versions.

Harvest festivals – like Lammas (first harvest in the summer) or the autumn festival of last harvest – may be easier to show to children in more rural districts. It could be possible to walk and watch harvesting in the fields. In towns and cities you are likely to have to use books to show young children images of the harvest, which has produced the food they can see displayed in the local church.

Responding to children's interest in a special event

The children may be fascinated by changes to familiar high street windows. Perhaps one shop does an impressive display of Eid cards and another showcases food special for a festival. Does one or more department stores in town do a special Christmas window, or other themed displays? Ask the manager if you can have leftover ribbons and shiny paper; they often just go out with the trash.

Listening to children and talking with them

The babies and youngest children will use these senses to take in the experience. Slightly older children may have comments or questions about what is happening and why. Over fours may also recall what happened 'last year' and ask if the apple bobbing and face painting of the previous Halloween will happen again.

Children may be actively involved in the preparations for some local events. Perhaps you all help out with the May Day decorations on your local green. The grown-ups will fix the full size maypole, but a smaller

version may be available for children. Some young boys and girls will have questions about how the pole is being fixed, or what will happen with all the ribbons.

Recall that you are not trying to get young children to understand everything about a festival or a faith-related celebration from this single event. It is inevitable that young children will take away simple messages, but you want them to be fairly accurate

Were children able to make sense of the main idea behind a harvest festival – especially if there is no visible harvest in your area? Or did the large number of tins and packets in the display muddle them? Did you get the balance right for children between the event and their choice to make something?

Learning about print in the neighbourhood

As well as all the other sights in your local area, there will be many examples of meaningful print: letters, words, logos and numbers. Young children are on a learning journey for literacy and numeracy and supportive adults offer experiences that help girls and boys to make sense of the abstract nature of written symbols. There will be many examples of written signs, but also visual imagery like one way signs or notices directed by pedestrians.

What do you need to do beforehand?

If you know that some children are already well aware of different numbers, then you could take out a small group with the simple plan of, "Let's spot as many numbers as we can on the way to the high street and back again". Depending on what children would like, you (or they) could be recording the numbers in a little notebook, or they might like to take photos, that could be made into a display later.

Exploring written material and logos can be intriguing with a little bit more preparation. You will have become familiar with the many different examples of written language in your neighbourhood. Take a wide range of photos of numbers, written notices, logos, road signs or symbols in the pavement like that for a cycling lane. You could collect these images during other local outings with the children. Enlist children's help, if they wish, to print and organise the sets of images you will use.

Print up five or six different types of image and have enough copies for each pair of children with an adult. Explain to the children that, today, you are going out 'spotting things'. Before you all go out, take time to look closely at the photos together. Listen to what the children have to say; their comments will give you a good idea of which images may be harder for them to find.

Perhaps some children have already shown you that they recognise the distinctive logo of a fast food chain or know enough about the idea of writing to ask, "What does that say?" about a notice in the park. Of course, you respond to children's spontaneous comments within any local trip. However, you could organise an outing when your main plan is to spot meaningful symbols in your neighbourhood.

The details of this outing will depend on individual children's current understanding. Under threes will not be making any sense of letters or numbers. However, they will be alert to other visual clues that you are about to reach the market or that this building is the library. Some older threes and the fours have started to realise as well as saying words out loud we can also write them down. They may still have to unravel that the meaningful squiggles they see can be numbers rather than letters.

An opportunity to learn about meaningful print and symbols

Three-year-olds may already be adept at counting objects in front of them, but understanding single written numbers is a different level of understanding. The first examples that seize children's attention will be part of first-hand experiences. It might be the number of the tram that passes close to their nursery or the brass number on the outside of their home.

In a similar way, written words and other meaningful symbols come alive within children's personal experiences. It might be the sign with the name of the railway station where you take them to watch the trains. The logo of a familiar high street chain or the name of your local café may be a child's earliest foray into understanding written, as well as spoken, language. When children are actually in the local post office on a visit, then it seems likely to them that this notice says "post office".

Young children are also learning about consistent visual symbols, such as cycle path or one-way road signs – which give a message but do not necessarily include actual words.

Responding to children's interest in symbols

What has caught children's attention, if you try the more open-ended version of looking at print in the local neighbourhood? Maybe you realise that some children are very interested in vehicle number plates and have worked out that these have letters as well as numbers. Perhaps you have four-year-olds who are experts on different types of car or lorry. They want to share their knowledge with you in conversation. However, as you chat, it becomes clear that these children would appreciate the resources to make their own registration plates and extend the activities of their role play garage area.

Maybe some children become especially interested in the power of notices to tell you something, like opening times or the difference between 'entry' and 'exit'. Are there meaningful opportunities for children to choose to make notices back at nursery or within your home? Their current skills of meaningful mark making, or the letter-like shapes within emergent writing, will be used and extended within this kind of child-initiated activity.

In an ethnically diverse neighbourhood there will be written notices in a range of languages and maybe also in different scripts.

Were all the children able to grasp the basic concept of looking for a match with the image in their hand? Or do you now realise that some children need more experience of looking to tell 'same' and 'different'?

Maybe some children have looked at this notice board many times, but did not realise that it actually said something. Do you have some children who are more sharp-eyed than others? Are they able to scan the street or this bit of the common to spot the real thing that was shown in their photo? On the other hand, do some of their age peers struggle with careful looking and making a comparison?

Listening to children and talking with them

Perhaps some of your photos, once spotted, provoke an unexpected level of interest and comment from the children. Maybe some grown-ups do not pay attention to notices that they must be able to read. The children spotted the "No dogs" notice for the fenced play area, so why has that person gone in with her dog? Or these symbols tell us that walkers go this side and cyclists go on the other half of the wide path across the common. So what did that cyclist think he was doing on our side? Sometimes children may need further explanation about how to tell the 'do' signs from the 'don't'. Perhaps in this instance, the cyclist is on the correct path.

Some children may be familiar with the logo for high street shops or fast food chains. Perhaps they have not really noticed the written name as well. You may wonder with young children why some shops have a logo as well as a written name and some just have the name. You may also realise that some children are confused and believe that the logo is actually a letter or a word. These are alternative kinds of symbolic representation and young children have to learn, sometimes puzzle out, the differences.

It is very possible that this focussed outing will encourage comments from young children that extend your understanding of their family life.

Learning about building and road works

Building sites or road works are only dangerous places, if you go inside the outer fence or barrier. They are safe places for young children, accompanied by an adult, when you stay outside and look; you never enter the hard hat area. Some construction work starts with the demolition of an existing building; other projects may fill a previously empty site. Road works start with the disruption of digging up the road or pavement.

What do you need to do beforehand?

Perhaps your first awareness of the road works or the new building site arises within a local trip with a different aim. Children's attention was caught by men digging up the main road or tantalising glimpses of trucks at work on a building site. You promise that you will all come back for a much longer stand and stare. Perhaps you make a written reminder in your special notebook that children understand is your memory jogger, so important plans are not forgotten. Perhaps the over threes can be part of a discussion about the best day to go back to this sight.

Keep an eye on what is happening locally. You can check out the best viewing points. Is there a set of windows for viewing the building site? Some gaps in the boarded boundaries are set at a lower, child height as well as adult height. Some sites are best visible from the other side of the road. Check out the location of the site office. It is sometimes outside the main hard hat building site area and therefore is accessible for you and the children. They may have a full scale model of the office block or flats.

You could pop in and ask whether it would be alright to bring a small group of children on a given day. The answer may well be 'yes'. Check with the site office manager about the precise scale of the model in relation to the final building.

You may discover local road works or deep holes behind safety fencing while you are out locally with a different purpose. If you are a childminder then the children will probably want to ensure you pass by this sight on a regular basis, while it is still there. If you have children with you on different days of the week, you will plan that they all get a good view of this exciting hole in the ground and how the high street traffic has to wind around it. A small group out for another purpose may come back with exciting news about what is happening. You make plans for other children to have a good look.

An opportunity to learn about construction

These local events offer useful experiences of longer term projects – sometimes very long term – where young girls and boys can see significant changes over time in a familiar location. The demolition and

construction aspects are very likely to be of interest to all the children from the toddlers onwards. The experience, especially if you revisit over a period of time, helps children to appreciate the sequence of stages in constructing something as substantial as a block of flats or offices.

It will be possible for young children to extend their understanding of how buildings are constructed. You can often get a good view of the inner sections of a building, which are invisible once construction is complete. Children will have seen the foundations and then the skeleton structure around which the more familiar aspects of a building have to be constructed.

It does not have to be a new building to be of interest for a local outing. You and the children will be able to watch how the roof of the town hall is mended or the spire of your local church. Perhaps you can watch as a local house has its tiled or thatched roof removed and is then repaired or completely renewed. You may be able to catch sight of the scaffolding as it goes up or is taken down on any of these projects.

Responding to children's interest in construction

You may be aware that some children – girls as well as boys – are already keen builders with blocks and boxes. Many young children are intrigued by big vehicles like diggers and dump trucks. So, you may have some accurate expectations of what will catch children's eye and ear when you go to look at the

building site. However, you may need to extend your knowledge of big tracks beyond diggers and dump trucks. You may be sharing the words to respond to children's interests in cranes, scaffolding, hard hats and other protective clothing, pipes, excavators, or pneumatic drills.

Later, some children might want to develop, or add to, their own building site in the garden. Perhaps they want to build a huge mound of earth and place their own digger on top – just as you watched the real digger perched on top of a mini-mountain as it emptied earth.

Listening to children and talking with them

Many workers are friendly towards small groups of adults and children. When you visit road works in the high street there is more opportunity to talk with workers who are standing outside the fenced area, or who pause in their work to greet the children. If a child asks you a question about the hole and the pile of pipes close by, then take the opportunity to suggest, "Let's ask". Encourage the more confident children to ask their own question. Otherwise you can say for the group, "We're wondering why you've dug this big hole" or "Can you tell us, please – what are the enormous pipes for?"

These opportunities show young children how we talk with people we do not know, when it is an appropriate situation for having a conversation. Children do not benefit from the blunt message of, "We never talk with strangers", because that is manifestly untrue. You talk with people you do not know when you first visit a market stall or when the staff change in the post office.

If you visit the site office, then show children the scale model or full sketch of what this housing estate will look like when finished. Children may be intrigued that the model and the drawings are not for play; it is an important part of how grown-ups plan the details of something really big. Some children may want to add this planning stage to their own constructions.

Learning about different ways to travel in the local community

Young children discover how much can be seen and enjoyed within walking distance of your nursery or home. However, some local places of interest will be a little bit further. Southlands Kindergarten has regular outings in which a realistic plan is to walk to their nearest town centre, make purchases for teatime and then take the bus back.

If you have reasonable public transport in your neighbourhood, you could plan an outing in which the main experience is the bus, tram or train trip. Alternatively, maybe within walking distance you can reach the ferry that crosses the estuary and enjoy that out-and-back trip.

This outing needs clear planning about the role of the accompanying adults. Safety on public transport with even a small group of young children requires adults to be alert, but not fretful. It must very clear which children are the responsibility of which adult.

The group needs a front adult who will lead with her or his two children and tell the bus driver that a group is getting aboard. You can also tell the driver at which stop the group will alight. Another adult needs to be the backstop, counts children into the bus and says everyone is now aboard. A reverse procedure works when you alight, with a friendly 'thank you wave' to the driver.

What do you need to do beforehand?

Check the timetable for the frequency of the buses or exact timings of less frequent ferry crossings. Do you have any circular routes or up-and-back trips where the views are good for children? If you take the short ferry trip across the estuary, is there a suitable walking circuit on the other side, before your return journey? The lead adult should have travelled this route before the trip with children.

Check out the pricing for tickets for the form of transport you plan to use. It is likely that two under fives will be able to travel for free on the adult's ticket. A ratio of two children per adult is a safe option for the alertness needed for public transport trips. However, if you have over fives with you, they will need their own child-rate ticket.

Place the name of your nursery and phone number inside children's coat or other clothing. You never fix a label with the child's name which is visible to anyone.

An opportunity to learn about travelling by public transport

Some children may already travel on public transport with their family. For other children, it will be a novel experience to travel other than in the back of a car. It will be many years before young children travel independently. Yet, they will be competent and confident in the future, if they have stockpiled experience of using public transport with adults who keep them safe now.

Over more than one travel outing, young children begin to understand the idea of getting a ticket – for the adult but probably not for themselves as yet. They will learn about getting to the right bus or tram stop and whether someone has to wave down the bus to request it to stop. They will learn about keeping safe on a railway platform, well back from the edge.

With your full support, children learn about how to get on safely and how to get ready to alight at the correct stop. They will learn that there is a bell to press to communicate that you want the next bus stop. However, your train or tram stops everywhere, so you do not have to ask. As journeys become familiar, some children will learn the order of the stops or stations.

Responding to children's interest in forms of travel

If the main aim of the outing is to be able to look out, then you and the children need to settle into a seat and relish what they can see out of the window. Young children may initially simply be intrigued about getting on a bus or train.

Perhaps the children are most intrigued by a different visual perspective for a familiar sight. Maybe you are now travelling in a train along the embankment and up to now you have watched the trains from a favourite viewing point on the common. An up-and-back bus trip provides a different view from the return direction and children may also be keen to spot the main landmarks on the way back to the starting point.

Maybe you are only one stop along on the tram and children point out a little park or a fountain. You agree that it would be possible to walk to that place another day.

Have you learned about different ways to get around your local neighbourhood? Maybe you are genuinely able to say to the children that the tram trip was a new experience for you.

In what ways you are also reminded about not over-planning. The basic up and back tram ride was a delight to the children and they are all keen to repeat exactly the same trip. Maybe the children enjoyed their ferry trip but what they keep recalling was the walk to the jetty, when they saw a car limping along with a very noisy flat tyre. Their questions are mostly about this incident.

Listening to children and talking with them

Even those children who are relatively familiar with this form of public transport may have had limited opportunity to chat about how they think it all works.

Maybe some children have grasped that the words running along the digital display loop tell you about the next bus or train stop. However, they may believe that the disembodied voice belongs to the bus driver. However, on rail and underground trains, the driver does sometimes speak directly to passengers through the sound system. On a small ferry there may be no more than the actual voices of the crew giving announcements.

Perhaps children have been on a train before but not on the city tram. Both these forms of transport are on rails. Maybe the tram stops are raised from the ground, so they are like a platform. So what is the difference? Young boys and girls may comment as they realise that the tram goes though the streets close to cars and other forms of transport. But there are no other vehicles on the train tracks.

Young boys and girls are sometimes quiet at the time, and you wonder if they are taking in much at all. Then, a few days later, young children, even some threes, will perk up with, "You know that train we went on? Well...?" A question follows that shows that they have definitely been thinking about what you did earlier in the week.

Reflections on learning about the local community

Suppose you were making the case to other early years practitioners or team managers. Which anecdotes would you choose to highlight how your children extended their initial knowledge about the local area? What would you share about what children were enthused to do, what they said, or searching questions that they asked?

Just as important within your reflection, what have you learned? In what ways did you adjust your planning of outings? Did you find that you, or some of your colleagues, needed to rethink timings, or how much to include within a single local trip? Were you able to respond to unexpected sights and be flexible about the initial aim of the trip?

What have you learned about young boys and girls, who were already familiar to you, and their family life? Will you continue or repeat some of these experiences on a regular basis? Have any resources, provoked by children's interests from an outing, been integrated into the permanent play provision?

Finding out more

- Duckett, R. and Drummond, M.J. (2010) *Adventuring in early childhood education*. Sightlines Initiative http://www.sightlines-initiative.com/

- Lindon, J. (2011) *Too Safe for Their Own Good?* National Children's Bureau

- Lindon, J. (2009) *Parents as Partners*. Practical Pre-School Books

- Lindon, J. (2011) *Planning for Effective Early Learning*. Practical Pre-School Books

- OFSTED (2010) *Requirements for risk assessments*. www.ofsted.gov.uk/resources/factsheet-childcare-requirements-for-risk-assessments

- Rich, D. et al (2005) *First Hand Experience: What Matters to Children*. Rich Learning Opportunities

- Warden, C (2005) *The potential of a puddle*. Mindstretchers www.mindstretchers.co.uk

The early years frameworks across the UK vary in details, although have much in common.

- In England, the Early Years Foundation Stage is under review at the time of writing (early 2012). The proposed, revised framework is given in this link. www.education.gov.uk/consultations/index.cfm?action=conResults&consultationId=1747&external=no&menu=3

- Northern Ireland has two documents relevant to early childhood: CCEA (2011) Curricular Guidance for Pre-School Education. www.rewardinglearning.org.uk/curriculum/pre_school/index.asp
CCEA (2006) Understanding the Foundation Stage. www.nicurriculum.org.uk/docs/foundation_stage/UF_web.pdf

- Scotland also has two documents: Learning and Teaching Scotland (2010) *Pre-birth to Three: Positive Outcomes for Scotland's Children and Families*. www.ltscotland.org.uk/earlyyears
The Scottish Government (2008) *Curriculum for Excellence: Building the Curriculum 3 – A Framework for Learning and Teaching*. www.ltscotland.org.uk/buildingyourcurriculum/policycontext/btc/btc3.asp

- Wales currently has a framework relevant to over threes: Welsh Assembly (2008) *Framework for Children's Learning for 3 to 7-year-olds in Wales*. http://wales.gov.uk/topics/educationandskills/schoolshome/curriculuminwales/arevisedcurriculumforwales/foundationphase/?lang=en